Songs For Winter Rain

Songs For Winter Rain

Sophie Grace Chappell

. . .

ELLIPSIS IMPRINTS
2021

. . .

ELLIPSIS IMPRINTS
Durham, England

. . .

Twitter: @EllipsisImprint

Songs For Winter Rain
Print edition ISBN: 978-1-8380723-5-3

Cover design by Sara L. Uckelman. Cover photo by Sophie Grace Chappell.

First printing 2021

sponsae diu amicissimae

sponsa semper amica

dat donat dedicat

Contents

The Hill of Vision

Do not expect it in the green of May.
No cleanness in that growth that parturition
as pure as clean as death.

Nor in the bland and flyblown August sun,
in hot banality upon a balding lawn,
in non-event of sweltering desiccation.

Ignore October's blustering warm winds,
rain-rotted fruit let clog the orchard paths;
it brings no insight eaten.

But when the bloodline's thin as mercury
when ice flowers white on wood and stars the stream
then head up through the beeswarm of the snow
then climb the Hill of Vision.

18.01.00

Scan

My waving hands and arms
are caught in your searchlight's throb
they paddle away from the whiteness of your noise.

I am inspected by echoes
I am found in an attitude of prayer
my spine my signature tune.

So you may hear my picture,
you may see the sounds you bounce
off my bones or the four palpitating
chambers of my heart:

shadowy prognostics of the day
my monochrome thin frequencies
will bleed themselves into your roar of colour

13.04.95

Song for Summer Rain

Equidistant between the red dusk
of last night and today's hot dawn,
through thick silk curtains a new scent's coming,
a mid-June freshness of pollen-musk.

High in the dark hall, from the skylight,
there sounds a sudden hostile thrumming;
out in the dusty garden's moonlight
the gaunt grey owl pauses her calling:

on parched crop-fields, on thirsty lawns,
warm midnight rain is falling.

23.02.21

Elephants

Shadows on the sunset-lit savannah
of acacia trees, eighteen metres tall,
and snaky trunks that don't reach halfway up them.
Elephants are small.

The waterfalls of the wide Zambesi River
have wallows and waterholes for one and all:
four round feet doggy-paddle in barn-deep water.
Elephants are small.

Ears like palm-leaves catch, from the earth upwards,
bass frequencies from the far-off-distant call
of another herd that's twelve days' tramp to northwards.
Elephants are small.

Africa is a hugeness all around them,
a meadow continent-wide, unfenced, unwalled.
Yet man made war made famine has now found them.
Elephants are small.

Piano-keys and dominoes, umbrella-stands
and trophies for the hunter, spell their fall.
Elephants aren't big; but it is man
who, of all things, finds most ways to be small.

22.05.17

Rabbit Tracks

The white wood is woven with rabbit tracks:
with traces there all the year, but told only by snow.

Where panicky hearts that beat three times faster than ours
streaked underground away from huge vague threats
smelled instant in the wind,

see a lopsided cross, constellation of four dabbed prints,
repeated repeated repeated;

and think what standing sharpnesses,
what spaces of acute experience
othertimes buried from sight,
we their unknowing giants bring roofs crashing in on.

Earlham Park, Norwich,
21.02.96

Elsewhere

In Elsewhere rolls a river you do not know
down to an ocean you will never see.

Elsewhere's huge cities (nameless in your mind)
ring with a million arguments you're not in.

In Elsewhere a stray dog barks, but you don't hear it.
Its tautened nights, lit with ambiguous light
from the other side of your moon, are nothing to you.

But unconceive yourself,
and Elsewhere's *here*.

28.01.96

Start the Day

Begin again. From radios reconstruct
the murmuring beat of synthesised Today,
teeth brushed and laces tied and shirt-flaps tucked.

"Think hard: today responsibilities ducked"
(so counselling radio-rabbis blandly say)
"begin again."
                    Thus radio reconstructs

your earthly freight, your world news, and your luck,
it clothes the naked night in work's serge grey
with teeth brushed, laces tied and shirt-flaps tucked.

Night's dreams were a child's chaos, were thumbs sucked
for comfort from the fear of yawning day
begun again, a radios' re-construct,

where pointless thoughts and tameless wants are chucked
like yesterday's pyjamas, for the day's
teeth brushed and laces tied and shirt-flaps tucked.

Though hope's a child that won't grow up, its rucked
and shaving-mirror face, forty if a day,
begins again, to radios, to construct
teeth brushed and laces tied and shirt-flaps tucked.

12.12.88

Oxford Out of Term

The reckless heartfelt alliances, the smart things said,
the coffee-euphoric, late-night theories mastered:

in the intimate space between two bending heads
in a solitary breeze in an empty cloister,

on green baize staple-pierced, behind glassless shutters,
the last of last term's students' posters flutter.

27.01.89

Another Pair of Eyes

Another fortnight
one more inch of size
another week passed and
faint flickering butterflies,
messages from a dim beyond
within;

another month
another doctor's visit
an other growth
an other sentience in it;

another springing life's
first traces, like spring's first green bracken-tips unfurled;
blank-slate innocent, glistening in the dark,
another pair of eyes,
another sizeless viewpoint on the world.

03.02.96

Enlargement

The world's the space of wills. Irruption into it
will be new space, imperiously shaped
by some still hidden daemon, for itself,
the absorbent playing vulnerable self
that was not there before. And pinks and blues
and frogs and ducklings all await its call.
Stern small feet kick-press a stomach wall.

05.09.93

Slaidburn

Pennine rain and Pennine space and light
on vacant wet and brindled Pennine moors,
on damp woods ghosted over by Pennine mists,
on the curving clear steel muscle of the river,

in sunlight's brief extravagance defined
the shapeless heather endlessnesses

as suddenly and for one moment *mine*,
fully mine and fully mine alone,
my Northland,
my own country

Cycling from Slaidburn to Cross of Greet
11.11.96

The Uncanniest Stereo

Passing tower blocks at night, from below,
all their windows open,

or jumping down the steps
in some Hall of Res.,

your eye, your ear may catch
what goes through us all

like universal truth:
the uncanniest stereo

of all those televisions
showing, shouting the same in perfect sync.

20.01.89

Bowland

Winding slowly northwards, vaguely lost
in grey october country, through the midst
of smoky indistinctness of the hills.

Though mirror-river shape the slickskin beech
arching leaf for leaf,
reflection spills

till out of blurs and shifts
comes clarity:
the sun on the road to the sea
upon the hills.

Cycling from Whitewell to Lee Fell
26.10.96

Ghoul

On a clear but moonless night
(midnight blue between
black shapes of undrawn curtains)
I will slide into your dream.
Do not attempt to move.
My smile is pallid, formal, shows my teeth;
my soft laugh is a dry, well-mannered cough.
I smile because
as I am sure you realise
you're trapped.

Yes, do turn to the wall if it will help you,
or (to be more exact) if you think it helps;
do wrestle the heavy blankets over you,
to draw around your head and (ah) your throat
the dulling warmth of slumber.
Then, absolute silence seems your best chance.
Like a game: the first one to break it is out?
But, you see, you lose
because you breathe.
Nor will your blankets keep out
my fingers
my teeth
insubstantial.

And now it is time to begin. First, reactions.
Perhaps you can reach the light-switch on the wall
(you know where it is, you can see it in your head)
perhaps you can reach the switch before I reach you.
Perhaps: but, as you're aware,
the light-switch is
behind me.

20.02.87

Middle Earth

Witches lived by the pond in the Forestry once:
no bomb-site then, but ancient, unplumbed, elven.
Those summer-meadows' hay, those stands of spruce,
tangled and dry-scented, were our warren:
filled with our stealth, held monsters and sharp wonders,
strange painted devils for the eye of childhood,
held magic, black or white, or of as many colours
as Saruman's cloak in the story.
So for us
green hills and hillsides, Lancashire rain and wind,
gained faces of our fantasy, were turned into
the battleplace of armies long ago:
and chimneys, roads, and rooftops there below
became a makebelieve scarce worth our glances
while marvellous the runes and cognizances
of intricately-patterned dense-wrought shields
shone and flashed upon our empty fields.

Hawkshaw, Lancashire
for Janet Ironfield
20.05.87

Presents

Sunlight on the orchard that my mother knew
and sunlight on the balcony where my grandmother sat
and sunlight that unendingly reinterprets
the rough rock-garden steps of grey horned limestone
where my small daughter climbs.

And all this I have always known and always had
I can know only now: can only have
for this one present.

Sit light to what is given, for
you do not pass this way again.

Seawood House, Kent's Bank, Lancashire
24.03.96

Cartmel

Old white limestone fluted by fossil seas
surprises as grey walls to Cartmel fields,
as thin irregular houses, and the Priory:

jackdawed lantern-tower and angled nave
with blunt grace like a castle's, Borders-strong,
seen round each corner, high over roofs in the lanes.

Sharp-lined hills stand northwards, south the sea,
over the fell-top, down the six-foot stream.
Blown from the Bay, the blue curtains of oncoming rain.

28.05.87

At Nought I Was Your Hidden Signature

At nought I was your hidden signature,
the knotting in your side,
your clotting pulse.
We needed no communication
being a single thought.

At flailing four
you answered all my questions.
At self-consumed fourteen
I stonewalled all of yours.

At twenty-four I left.
We met to talk, but sometimes telephoned.
Later we telephoned, but sometimes met.

And now at forty-four
a knot is in my side,
a catch is in my pulse
that is not you.

What is you is a ten-year dust of ash
in the roots in the straggling nettle-grass
in a garden itself to be burned.

Yet my phone still promises you on the other end
if I could just find the number.

GPS
30.11.1937–13.12.1989
27.05.10

Album

I've stapled the past down:
it's firmly collected into a book at home.
There it all is in black and white,
Agfacolours and Kodachromes,

3D colours in 2D prints,
sometimes catching thought's fine movements:
other times awkward poses, paperflat smiles
merely conceal.

Time's focus slips the pain and blurs delight,
the vivid colours and confusions
have all faded.

I can't remember much about these, now,
except the when and where.

21.08.87

Music Recalled

Music is what gives forms to the unconscious:
forgotten music finally played again
decodes from subliminal shapes a thought and a feel
I had not remembered having;

it reopens a scent-capsule of experience,
freeze-frames for good one single carriage window
out of the blurring rush of the storming train
of months and weeks and days and hours and minutes:

it fixes, uniquely, how it smelt and sounded
to be then, and to be listening to this.

The past is an abstraction, and past's self unknown;
but beating now and here, in this same music,
the laughing heart of then and there is caught,
for one moment of pure precision, in pin-sharp focus:
delightful the tricks the human mind plays on us.

24.12.95

Seawood

Close up the house. Strip coat- and key-rack clear.
Enshroud in dust-sheets the cracked chandelier.
Break stiff carpets from new-echoing floorboards, break
the wandering webs old cellars and bookshelves make.

Close up the house and count in every key.
Throw out the greyed and paled photography.
Peel bleached stickers from kids' windows. Turn the lock
the last time on the sun-porch and the silenced clock.

Close up the house and in an envelope seal
the keys to fifty years of thought and feel.
Now all we dreamed here, everything said and done,
goes north of the north wind, west of the setting sun.

Seawood House
Kent's Bank, Lancashire
1959–2012
09.12.09

Unanswered

An elm case stands, lid sealed, before brown drapes;
Enigma's tear-throb swells from your Top Classics tape.
Your winged armchair's empty now. You have left all this,
and nothing seems as serious as it is.

Once you'd drive me round late-sixties building sites
(new-car smell, *Sergeant Pepper*, rare Lancashire sun).
You'd answer all questions, set the whole world to rights,
explain to me rainfall during a change of lights,
get Darwin cleared up by the end of my half-term's run.

But I didn't just *have* questions. Question is what I was,
and Question I kept being, right up to this loss
by which both question and answer burn to nonentity,
vanish like *Cymbeline*'s words I said as solemnity.

I write all my questions down. But I leave them unsent
to pester what slept in you years; or was even then dead.
Always with us now each gift-cheque remains unspent,
always with us now what matters remains unsaid.

WGDC
11.4.35–24.12.19
13.02.21

The Disconnect Absolute

You wake up not knowing the time
you wake up not knowing the date
you wake up not knowing the century
or which of all these is your body,
forgetting the taste of yourself
and the reason the minotaur grief
                              slinks through your cellars.

Blindly you move to the window
shake through the pall-thick curtains
blindly you drink up outside
you drink up the bone-thin moon and the ghost-blue garden
you drink up the silver track on the scales of the sea.

The stuck record that fills your head with angular noise
plays on regardless of you.
The machinery of pain that you are involved in
it has no off-switch.
You do not notice
how you get back to bed.

The disconnect absolute
the bone-thin moon, the blue garden
all this will be gone in the morning
but not your loss.

26.12.08

Nostos

> *Get thee out of thy country...*
> *unto a land that I will shew thee*

Leave your homes here for your truer home.
Leave your hills (their mists around your heart)
for those hills whence your mists of longing start
though you have never come.
                     Mist-lifting day
will turn your face toward the homeward way.

Leave your work unfinished.
                     There is time,
where you are going, for the weaving mind
to make and remake reasoning and rhyme
a perfectness remaining undiminished.
To find as diamond what is lost as clay
turn your face and walk the homeward way.

And leave your friends.
                     One only you require,
that lover whose fierce heat etched in you's fire
that moulds your melting gold to bride-ring bends.
From marriage known to Marriage none can say
turn your face and take the homeward way.

Estranged by this sweet sudden discontent
shake off all exile-lands. Your time is spent
of wandering the mazes of life's Lent:
Easter calls you straight from every stray.
Rejoice and turn your face the homeward way.

4–5.3.98

Assumption

Mother of all on high,
pray for us yet

Nothing is left. The world's a corridor,
vacant, echoing the great ones' passage through.
It is closed doors in rows: behind them, murmuring
of a second generation's other businesses.
Nothing is left me here.

Once I felt the kick of God within:
nothing else seems great once that has been.

Your will is done,
and henceforth I will be
a silent smiling lady in a tapestry.

Your will is done,
and henceforth I am known
as a painted tiptoe figure in a pointed arch of stone.

Your will be done:
henceforth I watch with all
God's heroes in their sad unsleeping vigil
for earth's ball.

3–5.3.96

By This Time of Day

By this time of day, perhaps, you are
combing your hair.
You are pouring your morning tea
in another city.

And I stranded in this one
watch for the post.

28.08.98

Breakfast in Bed

Is eleven years' length too long for a conversation?
After so long, has every good line been said?
Does our contract need undecennial renegotiation?
Believing not, I bring you breakfast in bed.

Is every steady a frozen situation?
Are stones of indifference hardened from gift-bread?
Does love, in short, know time's devaluation?
Believing not, I bring you breakfast in bed.

For Claudia, 27.08.99
01.09.99

Keep Away From Buses

Given the overlapping
of our living that has happened,

given there's no reshaping
the once-only we're still making,

given all my bearings
would swing lost without your northing,

here is what I'm asking
you're not gambling or risking:

Save the lives of spiders
Don't walk under ladders
Don't change plugged-in fuses
Keep away from buses.

22.07.06

The Right Train

I've done some bad things and I've done some mad things.
I've done some things that got me in the stew.
Many of my options are not for sane adoption;
but I did a good thing when I married you.

Some people's choices are based on hearing voices.
Some read the stars, or the leaves in their Typhoo.
I treat life's junctions with minimal compunction;
but I took the right fork when I married you.

We have shared the sunlight,
                              and the sudden-failed umbrella.
We have sat out winters that stormed out of the blue.
Warmth drives branches upwards; cold pushes roots deeper.
What would I have done, if I hadn't married you?

Life is all alternatives, but hopeless information.
Unmarked and unsignalled, and too many for clear view,
trains line every platform through
                              the vastness of life's station;
but I caught the right train the day I married you.

For Claudia,
24.09.01

Two Pets

The power of human sight. The hanging hawk
Is only awaiting prey, but turns, observed,
To picture, image, symbol; becomes *framed*.
The power of human focus, of the rapt attent
That constellates the sky and names the species,
That populates the peaceful empty fields
Quiet with cow-pats and the small life of birds.

Or how a blank-eyed pebble-turning fish,
Bobbing in plastic weeds its simple scales,
Or furtive exoskeletal invertebrate,
Six legs and mouth-parts, stalking unawares
Within a human ten-year-old's arc-light awareness,
Is turned into a burning-point of love;
Is seen and by this concentration made
Something very good.

For Róisín and Thalia, pet-owners,
28.2.11

Glen Living

A river can run a thousand years through rock
not altering its course but only deepening it:
not so on the aimless free-meandering plain.

A farmer can lose a decade on one slope,
sink in one gorse-choked scarp a half-century's sweat,
yet not grudge the son who left all his random gain.

Think then how deep this glen goes in those who home here,
whose thought's this forest, this skyline their subconscious,
whose dream is this buzzard's wheel on this heathered
	moraine.

Tarfside, Glen Esk,
14.9.03

The Exiles

Still the blood is strong.

There every foot of field-end matters,
each river-pool is itself;
every stone is a sacred standing stone,
every hill a *sith* of the old ones;
here each street is the same
for mile after mile.

It only feels like what they had cannot be lost.
It only feels abiding unchanging home.
The bulldozer and the eviction writ,
north and south, work the same.

They walked into London's sameness
with heather-stalks still in their socks,
the plough-callus still on the insides of their thumbs,
the mark of the sheep-tick still fading behind the knee.

Kincardine O'Neil, Aberdeenshire,
07.11.08

Leaving Dundee

We build lives where we can: in factory towns
or willow-hollows on the dusty Downs,
in sandstone's gold or brick's suburban browns.
Roots anywhere are preferable to none:
your roots grew best beneath a late-night sun.

Mountains on one side and multis on the other,
harsh in its welcoming yet brusquely kind—
home of the friend sticks closer than a brother,
town of the tunes stick longest in your mind—
this is where you were kicked down, then recovered,
hope-enticed on, then tripped up from behind.

You know the line's first bend will end the scene,
your River and your wooded hills be gone,
your living places turn to what has been.
The diminutions of the South

　　　　　　　　　　　are coming on.

19.12.03

Sunday Morning, Edinburgh

Scrubbed Calvinist whinstone, grey as a Sabbath suit,
erupts (but in orderly fashion) into washed skies;
a wet dark stone, with a dour glint

                    in the sunlight.

Empty the spaces for cars; the foolish parking meters
stand idle, unprofitable; locked are the comfortless pubs;
the blinds on the actuary's office

                    bounce sunlight.

But below on a bistro pavement in the Grassmarket,
loud voices and Dayglo colours and avid movement
where Italian teenagers gulp down espresso

                    and sunlight.

Castle Hill, Edinburgh
12.03.91

Sunday Evening, Dundee Law

In dusk-glow at the War Memorial
dazed smokers lean on churning lurid cars,
review the week.

Beyond the huddled smirr-grey tenements,
amid the ancient chaos of the sea,
the Bell Rock starts its blink.

The Chinese lantern of a rain-fat cumulus
mirrored in still River
flows on by.

Always comes the rainbow, always, after storms,
the washed-clear and forgiven
cloud-lit sky.

09.03.08

How the Light Gets In

The light of all lights dazzles in our dark;
we shut our eyes.
The truth of all truths reasons with our hearts
blocked by our lies.
The joy of all joys asks us to dance, but we
prefer to grieve.
The king of all kings waits on us, but we're
too proud to receive.

Why then was he born in a cowshed?
That's where there was space.
And why was he born to Mary?
Because she said yes.

25.12.11

Boxing Day Morning

Yesterday the feast
today the penance

yesterday the spree
today the dearth

yesterday reunions—ex-wife, ex-child, ex-brother—
today we lick new hurts,
old lovers who know too well where to wound each other.

The hint-gift tracksuit waits, but it's too wet to bother.
A sea of wrapping-paper stretches door to hearth.

But lift your wine-furred eyes above the earth,
above our lost cold dawn, chill-drizzle-dim,
see Christ enthroned among the golden seraphim.

26.12.07

Ash Wednesday

As humans do here what they've so long done
the bitter spices burn in silver mists;
around the grandmother's knees the toddler twists,
warm hands playing candle-shadows on cold stone.

The two-thousand-year-old pain is here remembered
that stands for our earliest and our latest wrongs:
in the stillness remade generations-long,
offered foreheads, lined or smooth, are crossed with embers.

And there is time while a tall taper burns
to look along the pews to left and right,
to ask how long yet each of us still might
remember we are dust and to dust return.

Some of us present can remember when
they wore this lent ash sixty years past or more.
How many times have I done this before?
How many times will I do this again?

Exeter Cathedral
For Christopher Gill

Vigil Of Easter

The blackbird sang all night.
Secret in the dark, it promised dawn.
It whistled and mused on laughter after tears,
on the sweet lucidity of just-passed rain;

it chirped dew on hawthorn-buds and a springing rose,
green fields swum upwards from a rout of clouds,
the sad tired motions of a tiring mind
brought rest.
         It sang all out of time.
But now day's come, and the oldest rounds resume,
still the blackbird sings so sweet on the emptied tomb.

Easter Monday 2016

Carse of Stirling

For a moment of roadside relief just past Thornhill
you clunk from the car and you hope nothing else goes by:

and there on the verge, as the first frosty inklings of dawn
grope at the giant flat fields and the stands of Scots pine,
you watch as the curlews sweep and the lapwings spiral
out of the night-chill's thigh-mists into the sky.

Then you jump back in and you blow
                                on your trembling hands;
you slam in a Waterboys tape and you make the car fly,

shooting the corners like rapids to where Ben Ledi—
brindled by snow-melt, pastelled by soft morning rain—
comes sudden a gift of vision to the eye.

And so you keep going.
You have been heading, you are heading still,
towards these very same hills
for all of your life.

01.02.04

Glen Lui

You have never been in this place before
or even if you have it was different then.

The bright ragged pastures, when they speak to you,
speak with the curlew's voice;
          the clumsy pheasant,
lost somewhere on the pine wood's echoing slopes
in the holiday light and space of an April day,
fluffs yet another gear-change.
         From the gorse's
sheep-dunged mazes by the river, filled
with the sharp small halleluias of the wren,
the sun breathes warm and misty coconut.

Above the resinous wood hang the waterfalls.
Behind every glen-noise
        silence of a hill.

You will never be in this place again
or even if you are it will be different.

11.02.97

Allt a' Mhuillin, April

For the first time, the birchwood *not* by night,
path-bogs *not* sealed by corrugated ice;
for the first time, pied wagtails in the corries.
Pink sunshine slants through innocuous sleet-flurries.

Here on the Hut's rock-seats, snow-stripped, sun-warmed—
was it here we half-froze in the January storm?
Where the crampon drives through slush to brown-baked
      scree—
was that our icefall-route in February?

Did we tread here a snow that none had trod?
Did we glimpse here the hidden face of God?

Torlundy to Coire Leis
08.04.06

The Tors of Ben Avon

The tors of Ben Avon are elephants in seeming:
lounge in the sun on the sculpted dusty brae
two thousand feet above the empty glen,
snooty-alone or in queued-friendly baggage-trains,

a baggy-rounded squatting granite haunch
a hidden flange of mica-flapping ear
a sudden unlikely air-aspiring trunk.

The picture is made but no one here to see
no one but me to frame it as unframed.
So still you can hear God breathing.

East and West Meur Gorm Craigs, Ben Avon
21.04.11

Cue Music, Cue Eagles

The moment when the cloud unveils the moon,
the moment when the mist unveils the lochan,

the slate-blue rain-light on another hill,
the rainbowed waterfall above the rowan,

the summit-shattering winds and the hammering heart:

Cue music. Cue eagles.

Carn nan Gobhar,
Glen Strathfarrar, Invernessshire
30.06.96

The Vanishing

Hidden in you as the sleeping deer is hidden
warm in the highest cairn of the furthest hill,

I am snow-bound, thin-air-remote, unwatched
by the spies of the woodsmoke glens.

Or I am barred and locked, your secret garden: sealed
with soft flowers' fragrance, quiet rumours of water,

rumours relayed over blank and roughcast walls
that shut in the shining green, the sunburst lawns;

and all that bustles beyond our walls goes by
my paradise and pleasance of your joy.

Or fast in your arms, I sleep the sleep of dreams
in the deepest bed in the house of the perfect eaves.

He who dwells in the shelter of the Most High
She who rests in the shadow of the Almighty

                     disappears.

                                      26.06.98

Before An Icon

How little changes. Delight is always there,
waiting for us to fit it to our grasp
as it awaited her. And suffering is unending;
the contours of old pain etched in her face
are new in ours.
Prayers of healing, implorings of release
cannot go out of date
so long as birth and death are still our boundary-marks;
that long the Holy City,
the beautiful, the forsaken,
will still remain a ransacked ruin behind us,
will still remain a perfect dream ahead.

And the frightened soul like a sparrow
that flickers in mid-air suspense
over an infinite drop
under an infinite height

Chapel of the Icon of Mary the Mother of God,
Great St Bartholomew's Church, West Smithfield, City of London,
2.12.08

Bride

In the selfsame point that the
soul is made sensual is the City
of God ordained to it without end.

I give you my virgin white:
My blue-shadowed snows, my walled gardens,
My blank pages whereon you shall write
When I give you my virgin white.

You give me your spectrum-white:
You kaleidoscope all my colours
To one simple vision of light
In your prism-, your spectrum-white.

I give you my bridal white:
White, silk-sheened, frill-intricate lace
Grace has broidered for your desire's sight
In our ache of delight face to face
When I give you my bridal white.

21–22.05.98

The Box

My love met me within a darkened wood
where no light was: I knew her by her hand:
but my grip slipped, her presence vanished, and
till dripping dawn I waited where I stood.

I saw my love upon a city street,
amid a thousand others gave her chase:
I found her longed-for look in many a face,
ten-score half-echoes, but not one complete.

I woke and washed and worried at my error,
a looking-glass behind me and before me;
ninety-nine times repeated there I saw me—
and then *her* image in the hundredth mirror.

But my quest and her trail alike turned cold.
I've put my memories of her in a box
to hide inside a drawerful of socks
and finger through when all grows stale and old,

and I have lost the living patterns of
her stance, her grace, her glance so once adored;
have settled for sure less not dubious more,
have lived as if I was not made for love.

When I began so filled with venturous fire
how comes my world to dust and grit and sweat?
Is real-but-paltry really all we get?
How can we live so wide of heart's desire?

09.12.07

The Mirror

> ἡμεῖς δὲ πάντες ἀνακεκαλυμμένῳ
> προσώπῳ τὴν δόξαν Κυρίου
> κατοπτριζόμενοι τὴν αὐτὴν εἰκόνα
> μεταμορφούμεθα ἀπὸ δόξης εἰς
> δόξαν.
>
> Paul of Tarsus, 2 Cor. 3:18

I am a mirror
faced towards the wall
I bounce no sight

I am a mirror
angled into earth
I give no light

I am a mirror
stained and cracked and smeared
my glance is dim

I am a mirror
point me at my source
and I blaze Him.

This is the famous glass
that turneth all.

16.01.06

Song of Songs

CHRISTIAN

I'd say when I was eight I loved you first,
except that that sweet start of longing, felt
sweet lack, no sooner felt than filled,
played full what countless younger plays rehearsed.

LOVER

All streams will flow to one unchanging main,
the sea of love that seals, shapes, and begins you.
You were not formed before my love was in you;
there is no start in you that is not mine.

CHRISTIAN

Or say I loved you first when I was twenty—
and truly then our streams were in sweet flood,
and, half my life ago, our love was good:
and yet a mere half-measure of now's plenty.

LOVER

You're made of the dust of stars, as fine as sand.
In me you find a home in infinite space.
My love, my spring of delight, my secret place,
there was no start, and there will be no end.

25.12.07

West Hedleyhope

Fat green grass feeds on glinting dusty spicules;
blowsy burdocks glut the barbed-wire meadows.
These briars grow out of tarmacked anthracite.

The miners' pigeon-pens are empty now.
A wind-farm struts the moor-ridge. Chimneys seep
a black smoke still; but of coal that came by ship.

And in the littered play-park new graffiti
resurfaces old angers long-defeated,
the Red Flags oversprayed into Union Jacks.

I climb to the moor-ridge, join the Roman road,
head on towards the vanishing point of England.

Cycling Dere Street, County Durham
                                    11.05.17

Another Spring

Without you to consult about it
I have chosen a shade of blue
to spring-repaint the salt-blistered window-frames
around what, all these years, were your favourite views.

And now the full-grown rosemary-shrubs we planted,
dancing in the rough April wind's renew,
sun-reflection-rippled at high tide, bee-haunted,
are also flowering blue.

Another spring is moving over these dead old leaves,
but this time, for the first time,
I see it without you.

Pontac, St. Clement, Jersey
05.04.12

Had Enough

I'm tired of myself and my moods,
Of being controlled by my rages;
By old sorrow that festers and broods,
By the baggage of ages and ages;
My own spite that must settle its scores,
My stale repertoire of poses and masks.
I don't think I want to be me any more.
Please can you give me an easier task?

If I hadn't been me
I'd not have hurt B
Or offended A
Or driven C away;

If I hadn't been me
I'd have made it with D
Not split up with E
Thawed the cold war with F;
Almost certainly G
Would never have left;

My friendship with H would be just as before
Had my struggles with I not now led me to ask:
I don't think I want to be me any more.
Couldn't you give me an easier task?

Somewhere out there is a character simple,
A straight-up persona with no traps or wrinkles,
A cold shower of simplicity in which I'd bask,
All complexes kicked off outside the door:
Can't I be that, and not me any more?
Wouldn't I find that an easier task?

19.01.08

Christmas Wishes

By popular request
Captain Hook will replace his hook with a tickly feather
        duster
and pass around the gobstoppers with the Lost Boys.
As a seasonal gesture
the Daleks will change their war-cry to "Have a nice day"
and The Joker will actually tell one.

By popular request
global warming will global cool
and the beef-farms of the Amazon will be turned back into
        rain-forests.
As a seasonal gesture
entropy will take a holiday in St Tropez
and dropped toast will consistently fall butter side up.

By popular request
and as a seasonal gesture
lost children will be found
and brutal feuds be ended;
the inconsolable will be consoled,
the outcast and downcast be welcomed in,

and something unthinkably and invisibly vast
will pass into a space
invisibly small.

If you only make one wish this Christmastide
make sure it's for something impossible.

18.12.07

The desire of all nations shall come
Haggai 2.7

St George

Heraldic-taut white-shining-armour knight
over a honey-stone font.

Mailed foot pressing down on the neck of the vanquished
      beast,
a leaning twist on the righteous skewering spear:
one shafting thrust ends the triumphing hero's hunt.

Thus is the slick gross leathery-wingèd dragon
poison-green and stone-cold-eye malicious
stamped out and erased
extirpated and excised
by our purified Christian Perseus
freed from sin.

So what is it Andromeda's temporary saviour misses?
How is it ice-chill heart and fire-lust rage
live on within?

St Michael at the Northgate, Oxford
(so not in fact St George, but never mind)
23.04.14

Buskers on Buchanan Street

To grey-suit minds set on trains
in grey-suit business streets
silky jazz unfolds from the sheets
in shimmering scarlet skeins.

Jumping the bars of the notes
transgressing performance space
a wee girl hides her face
as she donates.

14.12.07

A Prayer for My Daughter

Pour upon my daughter's face
all the rainstorm of your love:

while she shapes, blind oceans deep,
the ink-black element of sleep,

though the whirling earth may move,
cast a stillness on this place.

17.7.97

Spring Cleaning

Piano-playing would cause pittering in the hall,
a round grey face regarding you from the doorway:
watchful, semi-curious, companionable.

Opening the fridge caused a mini-stampede:
instantly there, periscoping on your feet,
whiskering aloft, wide-eyed for broccoli.

Kneel on the floor, and she would lollop to you,
nose on your knees, long ears spread out sideways to stroke,
fluff spiralling up the draughts from her blue-silk fur.

For six years I read and wrote in her calm mild presence,
paws out, head held high like a miniature sphinx,
or standing up to clap and wash her face,
or lounging on her side like a portrait-spaniel.

The house is empty now; it holds only humans.
This is the last clean that still turns up her pellets.
Maybe it's well not to feel too much for creatures
if there is this much to feel.

Vaisey the grey minilop, 1.9.2011–23.1.2018
25.01.18

Wherever You Walk

Wherever you walk
I'd be the walker beside you;
wherever you travel
I'd be the guard on your train;

whenever you sleep
I'd be the angel above you,
guiding your dreams
past the sheer cliffs of fall in the brain.

If I was God
I'd not let you out of my eyesight;
if I was God
you'd never feel lost at cold midnight;

if I was God
I would de-booby-trap every portal;

but I am not God,
I am only another lost mortal.

Off, then, on your journey
where I have no business to go;
off on your way
to make friends whom I'll never know;

your life will be different and yours
and mostly not about me;
my main part in it will be just
to be a good memory.

For Miriam, before her first long-distance journey alone
08.08.08

Taking Up Residence

Sunshine and a faint jazz-band
from Kelvin Park.
Black parental Beamers parked
and double-parked.

Rucksacks, boxes, crocks,
bags full of shoes.
Name-badged smiley second-years
on the fire-doors we bump through.

This small-big paint-smell space
is yours now for the year.
No blutack on the walls.
Are the fire-rules clear?

So that's it? And it's enough?
We'll meet up some time or other?
And what if there's only today
to say that we love each other?

Cairncross House, Kelvinhaugh, Glasgow
29.09.14

Tutela Praesens

When you smile at things, I will smile as well;
when sad, I'll try to smooth your tears away.
I'll listen—and laugh at—the jokes you tell,
will be your partisan in work and play.
I'll try to make a sweet peace where you dwell,
the wolves that prowl your porch, to shoo away;

but I am no closer than you to heaven, or hell.
I just watch, helpless-auspicious, over your way,
a fragile household god who will fail some day.

02.10.20

The Pole Star

The heavens rolled, the earth overturned beneath me.
Seas surged, whole continents cracked and broke in two.
One star stayed constant at the pole above me.
That star was you.

People came and people went around me.
Some friends proved useless; some unfriends turned true.
One friend stayed put to soar me and to ground me.
That friend was you.

I spin the globe; four thousand miles go by me;
I chase far snow-peaks, pierce thick forests through,
to find again that the where and who most tie me
are home and you.

For Claudia
Canmore, Alberta
31.08.2017

The Pigeons

Tram passengers huddle for warmth and scatter for privacy,
They preen their shoulders, peck at paper cups,
shake their heads at the snow days they see coming.
Above them on the gable the town's pigeons

huddle for warmth and scatter for privacy,
preen their shoulders, peck at the dead spring's seeds,
wait for the snow days when half of them will die.

But we who wait are us
and they are vermin.

Watch a fly clean its wings
Watch a hare wash her ears
Watch a professor polishing his glasses.

The wide world's weird and wild
But with our kin.

Life is one
and suffering is one
and pity and compassion must be one.

The Cathedral Café, Oslo
11.10.14

The Cyclist

The cyclist's ride depends upon
two air-pockets, two gaps of air:
on two round envelopes tight-blown,
on what's there by not being there.
On this cushion of nothing, through moonlight wood
or down the dim hill-pass at dawn,
whether coasting or climbing, the cyclist floats
on emptinesses that she leans on.

Old-time doctors attended deaths
with scales and with great care
to weigh before and after breath
was there, then no longer there.
But the soul weighs nothing (who'd say that it would?),
and every cyclist knows that
the machine feels *heavier*, and won't float,
before you have fixed the flat.

The time will come (it always comes)
when the air-pressure finally drops,
when the empty space seeps from those taut round drums,
when the pneumatic rolling stops.
Yet through forests clothed in spring's living green,
in their sweet breath, till then she will ride,
making somethings from nothings, invisibles seen,
and sweetness from being alive.

01.11.20

On Belay

Anyone else, in this, would be scared and cold
but then so are you.
All there is, is the drops above and below
and you in between them,
alone with last year's heather-root eagle's nest
and the dip of the aerial raven.
In your hand are the half-taut lines that twitch and shiver
and faint-relay a morse of watchful movement
from somewhere up above you.

Raw freeze in the icy maw of this dark vertical
yet across the glen, the deer drift up sun-pink snow.
Red trembles slightly and you pay out small.
You stamp and flake and stamp and flake and hear
grouse chuckle and scold, and the river run on for ever.
Here and now and nowhere and nowhen else.

This particular stillness in the ropes
means that he's at the crux
and the crux is going to be hard
and that he's looking at it and thinking how.

Anyone else, in this, would be cold and scared
and so are you.
The difference is that you're other things as well.

Angus glens, with Simon Richardson
20.01.18

Hopefall

From dawn to dusk—and earlier, and later—
we spun our new line up towards the skies,
shadows of movement in the greater silence,
a quiet but shared ardour in our eyes,
while sunlight danced from snow to loch to sea.

And then the got-it moment met our hope:
the angle fell away and the rest was white,
a walk-up to the summit, trailing ropes,
the black crag overcome, and the plan come right.

But if a fault appeared then and gaped open
and widened till it swallowed you and me,
tripped up, ensnared and swamped, so quickly taken—

that does not mean our partnership was broken;
does not annul the trust that set us free;
and does not take the sunlight from the sea.

In memory of Andy Nisbet and Steve Perry
Ben Hope, Sutherland, 05.02.19
08.02.19

Love Poem

My Lord draws me
a reluctant beloved
down from surface turmoil
to the still depths of his heart

17.01.84

The First Haiku of Spring

Haiku haiku hai
ku haiku haiku haiku
haiku haiku
ku

25.09.89

The Damage

Maybe we should do one another more damage.
I can't remember when I last left you crying.
Domesticated love's grown middle-aged;
young feral violence once came without trying.

14.01.89

Three Developments

"The Meadows", new houses
where hayfields and birds used to be.
"The Beeches", new houses
where they have cut down every tree.
"Sea View", where new houses
now block the old view of the sea.

05.10.18

Today the Sun Will Rise

Today the sun will rise
whether or not you see it;
dawn-light will transfigure cloud-skies
though your tired eyes may miss it;
new splendour will shape bright air
though you are far below it;
and God's love for you too will be there
whether or not you know it.

04.02.19

Up the Law

Up the Law
in the winter dark
an owl is calling
a snow is falling
in the dark.

08.02.18

Disenchanted

When you are young enough
all is light-haunted
dazzling stars shoot each moment
enchanting delight

Now you are old enough
to see disenchanted
but here's the illusion:
it was *then* you saw right.

31.01.14

Love's Phases

I
I want
I want you
I want you with me
I want you to be happy with me
I want you to be happy with me so long
I want you to be with me so long
I want you to be with me
I want you to be happy
I hope you will be happy
I hope you will be
So long
I hope
I

20.11.20

Spring Shower at Tulloch

The sun's emerging spreads
warm pungency of wet dog-rose
slantwise across the sleepers'
creosote airs.

19.07.96

The Night Before You Go Ice-Climbing

Your crampons are in your garage
Your axes are under your bed
Your gloves are in your sock-drawer
Your helmet is in your shed

Your heart is in your mouth.

21.12.16

In One Moment

A cemetery
a tomb
a place of death

is suddenly
in one blinding moment
a place of life.

Shalom.

07.10.83

Father to Daughter

I drive you to the station.
I unpack your bags for you
(you've packed too many)
I see you onto the train
you go away.

If there was more that I could do for you
then I would do it
but in so many ways you are on your own.

13.03.10

Sabbath

For six days the Lord did labour, and made the earth;
and on the seventh
He skulked inside unshaven with a Bible in His hand,
and scowled at the neighbours.

07.05.18

Vain

You call me vain
Yet every mirror I've ever approached
Had me in it;
Just like every rainbow I've seen
Centred on my face.
Coincidence?
I don't think so.

18.12.17

News

The change comes on so suddenly
the moment of transition
the phone or letter butts into
the same old stale position

you pick it up quite casually
not knowing what is in it
while clock-hands drag and dust-motes float
life changes in one minute

08.04.06

Parenting Skills

Bad parenting:
you go out of the house
so you can ignore your children.

Good parenting:
you stay in the house
so your children can ignore you.

11.11.03

The Children's Cemetery, Balgay

Parents' sentences on marble;
mildewed dolls beneath grown trees:
O you who mark the sparrow's fall,
did you not notice these?

25.08.06

January Sales

In the sales you mustn't miss
at the prices you can't beat
buy the things that you don't want
with the money you've not got.

01.01.99

Most Hills

Most hills should be climbed quite alone.
Could I do what cannot be done
and climb them alone-with-someone
then quite obviously you'd be the one.

23.04.11

Guest Room

In someone else's double bed
I compose myself
on what, at home, 's your side
then double-take.

31.07.09

Prayer at Baldowrie Symbol Stone

The Holy being still with us though unknown,
to keep your ever watching listening care
over indifferent lives and living air
set a strong good angel in this stone.

Baldowrie, Strathmore
27.12.03

Shakespearean Limericks

(i)   Not Juliet's family's strife
stopped her from being Romeo's wife;
     it was surfeit of suitors
     and ill-advised tutors
and doing for herself with a knife.

(ii)   Ant was playing sweet duets with Cleo:
their *thés-dansants* were *molto con brio.*
     But to 'Tavius' clasps
     she preferred little asps,
thus preventing him making a trio.

(iii)   Henry the Sixth's holy heart
lacked the courage a crown should impart;
     yet his reign wasn't brief—
     it endured past belief,
till the Yorks cut him into three parts.

(iv) Henry Fourth (the First Part) said, "That's that!
      Get a life! Be a prince, not a prat!"
            Hal replied, "Sure, don't worry, Dad,
            but where is the hurry, Dad?
      There's your whole Second Part before that."

 (v) "Let's sit down," said Richard the Second
      as Bolingbroke's destiny beckoned:
            "My holiday in Eire
            makes my last hopes threadbarer.
      Still, being King's worse than he's reckoned."

(vi) When *Bassanio* gets parasitic,
      Antonio is no fierce critic;
            but *Shylock* calls in debts
            and they *all* get upset.
      The whole play is anti-Semitic.

(vii) There are twins. They come in two pairs.
      Two are humble. Two give themselves airs.
            There's some fine to pay.
            Then the rest of the play
      is from Plautus; but frankly, who cares?

(viii) Hamlet, this noble young Dane,
       feels disdain for avuncular reign.
            When surprised at his post
            by his murdered pa's ghost,
       he sanely feigns mainly insane.

(ix)   "Who loves me the most?" cried King Lear.
Would Cordelia flatter? No fear.
    Her love was too pure.
    I am left feeling sure
this could all have been solved over beer.

(x)   Iago (conspicuously mellow,
Yet not really such a nice fellow)
    Proved less sweet, more lemoner,
    In the life of Desdemona,
And really fucked over Othello.

(xi)   The Duke pushes off for some leisure,
leaving Angelo guarding the treasure.
    He thinks he's the fella
    to take Isabella.
But she takes him—measure for measure.

Various idle moments, 1989–2020

Etienne Jodelle, Sonnet 30

Like one who, in the forest, has lost his road,
far from his way, far from sound or sight of friends;
like one who, caught in the war of great sea-winds,
freezes, does nothing but watch himself drown in the flood;

like one still afield when colourless night sucks the blood
from the gaudy noon's neck as the grey-drained daylight
        ends—
so I have lost road, light, and almost sense;
have lost that one object in which my most happiness stood.

Yet when men see again (these ills being gone),
in wood or sea or field, road, port, dawn,
they see those then-ills were less than this now-good.

I then, who was all of this while you were away,
forget, as soon as re-see your radiant day,
the black cold bite of night, storm, bitter wood.

Comme un qui s'est perdu dans la forest profonde,
Loing du chemin, d'orée et d'adresse et de gens;
Comme un qui, en la mer grosse d'horribles vens,
Se voit presque engloutir des grans vagues de l'onde;
Comme un qui erre au champs lorsque la nuict au monde
Ravit tout clarté, j'avais perdu long tems
Voye, route, et lumière et, presque avec le sens,
Perdu long tems l'object où plus mon heur se fonde.
Mais quand on voit (ayant ces maux finy leur tour)
Aux bois, en mer, aux champs, le bout, le port, le jour,
Ce bien présent plus grand que son mal on vient croire;
Moy doncq qui ay tout tel en vostre absence esté,
J'oublie, en revoyant vostre heureuse clarté,
Forest, tourmente et nuict, longue, orageuse, et noire.

Etienne Jodelle (1532–1573), *Les Amours*, apud Simone Weil, Cahiers XII 412
trans. *20.02.19*

Eheu fugaces

Our sorrow, Postumus, is time gone past,
lost years, sunk, buried, never to reseek.
Our prayers cannot postpone the wrinkled cheek
nor looming age. Death always wins at last.

Sacrifice him two thousand bulls a week,
dear Postumus—you'd only waste your breath.
No pleading stays the hand of the god of Death;
not even giants wade back, once crossed his creek.

For all of us, some day, that's all that's left:
no matter what our portion in this life—
fat kings or peasants inanition-rife—
we all will sail in Charon's one-way craft.

No help forgoing bloody warfare's strife,
pointless to heed some seer's "Avoid the sea".
No tricks nor hacks can fix mortality;
the fever-wind's not the real threat to your life.

Like it or not, that meandering stream you'll see,
the black sleek Cocytus, hell's languid river
where the Suppliants, damned, fill leaking pots for ever,
while Sisyphus strains at his stone eternally.

Like it or not, your home, your land, your lover—
you'll lose them all. Your saplings grew so fast,
now taller than you, and you they will outlast.
Your cypresses will be your grave's shade-cover;

your heir will drain your cellars to their last,
will break their locks for the brandy you kept as antique,
will ruin your lapis floors with the red-stain leak
of wines too fine for the high priests' fat repast.

Horace, *Carmina* 2.14
19.04.20

Rainer Maria Rilke, A Classical Torso of Apollo

The statue's head is lost. We cannot track
the fertile glance that ripened there. Even so
what's left's lit up like a ring of candles' glow,
in which his gaze on you, though thus cut back,

still keeps its brilliance. That alone is why
his breast-curve turns your sight, his smooth round joints
deflect a soft smile downwards, towards the point,
his being's centre, where conceptions lie.

And that is why he is not just maimed stone,
hacked short below the shoulders' seen-through zone;
and why he glistens like a wild beast's fur,

and overruns the boundaries of his form
as a star will, till his every part is blurred
into one looking at you.
            Be transformed.

11.01.20

Sophocles, *Trachiniae* 1264–1278

Attendants, take him up. And pity on me,
Pity and compassion on my plight,
All while the unpitying gods indifferently
Watch these things unfold under their sight.
They make us and they claim the name of fathers
Then stand afar and watch our suffering.

No one knows what the future time will offer;
The present time, for us, means suffering,
And for the gods means shame;
It means worse than any human suffering
For him on whom this doom of anguish came.

Girl, come away, and leave this house behind.
New shapes of enormous death now fill your mind,
Novelties of agony, pain beyond all use—
And nothing in all this that is not Zeus.

26.06.08

Catullus, 11

Furius and Aurelius, comrades of Catullus,
whether I go as far as the ends of India
where Ocean's shores, louder-sounding, thunderier,
boom with their breakers;

whether to soft Arabians or to the Caucasus,
to the Scythian savages, the archers of Iraq,
or where the Nile, septuplet river, turns dark
paddy-field marshes;

or if I climb over gelid Alpine passes;
step in the footsteps Caesars and Hannibals made;
cross the Rhine into Teuton forests; wade
to world's-end isle Britain—

wherever time might, at the whim
                            of their heavenly highnesses,
decree me for exile, I know you would also dare;
but all I ask's this. Go to Lesbia; bear
this brief, not good, message:

that she stands condemned to her Pretty-Boys' Club and
        her fantasies,
entangling them all at one time, three hundred in number,
loving not one of them truly, yet member by member
screwing them senseless.

And let her not sigh for return of her former love's gentleness.
His love's like the poppy that edges the meadow-side last,
stands like the poppy-stalk after the rust-blunt plough's
        passed
ripping the flower off.

16.05.87

Sappho, 31

He seems to me to be the high gods' peer,
that man who sits beside you, sits so near—
always so near. Your every word he hears,
all your sweet laughter;

he listens to you so calmly. Whereas I
am gasp-breath racing pulse when you're nearby,
am cannot-look-at-you, am tongue-is-tied
for hours after;

words fall away and atoms of fine flame
prickle across my skin with longing shame,
thunder-darkness takes my vision, and the same
removes my hearing;

and I am drenched in freezing sobbing sweat,
and I am palsy-rigid, trembling wet,
and I am hay in winter, still live yet
but snow-death nearing.

10.02.18

Catullus, 8

Hopeless Catullus, stop hoping for reprieve,
and recognise that what you know's died's dead.
Her sunlight quickened you, and now you grieve;

when she was loved like no one who has lived
you gladly followed where her bacchics led,
but now, Catullus, hope for no reprieve:

your childish games—the sweet-smile make-believe
you asked of her—at least were not gainsaid
while her light quickened you: but now you grieve.

Her soft Yes, now hard No beyond retrieve,
should harden you as well, barred from her bed,
hopeless. Catullus, don't hope for some reprieve;

be flint! Be steel! Don't beg what she won't give,
don't lick old wounds; outstubborn her instead.
"Your sunlight quickened me and now I grieve,

but, Lesbia, it's Catullus who now leaves:
he tired of you before, but never said.
Lesbia, hopeless, stop hoping for reprieve!

Bitch, what life is left you, when I leave?
Who will you find who'd choose to fill your bed?
My sunlight quickened you but now you'll grieve:

You'll never kiss me sleeping while I breathe
your name..."

        But oh, I bled, I bled, I bled:
Your sunlight quickened me, and now I bleed.
Hopeless, Catullus. Stop hoping for reprieve.

08.07.87

Horace, *Odes* 1.34

With Octavian in the thunderstorm

So many years I've left the gods alone
as they've left me alone; and I have kept
my world clear, rational, little, but my own;
huge underworld unreason, unroused, slept.

But I must re-dance pre-enlightened steps;
child's chaos roars back, all its winds re-blown.
For Jupiter, whose usual lightnings leapt
out of full clouds that crowd-thronged the on-high,

now burns white bolts down from a cloudless sky.
His clear-sky thunder rides the blank blue cleft,
his clear-sky lightning spills earth's streams, cracks stones;
this lightning pierces even to hell's depth;
he thunders here, and the Outer Ocean groans.

Jupiter lifts the low, casts down the high,
installs the nameless in the noble's throne.
Shrill Fortune strikes the king uncrowned, bereft,
shriek-laughs to plant that crown on one unknown.

17.05.17

Horace, *Odes* 3.15

Chloris, old Ibycus' wife
(and him on his uppers as well),
at your age, d'you think that your life-
style *ought* to be that of a belle?

Although you've one foot in the grave,
the other one's still minuetting
in Rome's smartest sets. Your behav-
iour's a cloud on its star-silvered setting—

you, a grandmother, clinging to Fashion!
Inch-thick make-up, to ape-up Pholoe!
But watch *her* ransacking men's passions
with her dark eyes, dark hair (yours is snowy)

and consider. With *you*, they're—polite;
with your *daughter*, they're at it like rabbits;
yet you flirt on gamely, in spite
of your manifest need of changed habits.

No, Chloris dear: take my advice:
bowls of roses, night dances, don't fit you
nor cocktails drained down to the ice.
Your gaiety's no longer nice.
Take up knitting. And try it *in situ.*

16.07.85

Aeschylus, Agamemnon 887–973

CLYTAEMESTRA

. . . Time has dried up the fountain of my tears;
those springs of pity, parched, don't even drip.
My eyes are strained and sore from endless watch,
from the tears I shed for the fires unlit for you
that brought no news, while my sleep's flimsy cover
was needled through by the small sharp shrill mosquito.
Every night the sufferings I saw
enringing you went on all night and more.
All that's endured and over. With grief mending
I hail you as the watchdog of our steading;
as the mainstay of our ship; as our strong tower
holding our roof up; as sole heir empowered,
unlooked-for land in sight of those lost in the ocean,
still brightness rising from dark storm's commotion,
a desert traveller's first sight of fresh water in motion.
These epithets I think him worthy of;
though after all this, we must ward off the envy Above.

But now, dear head,
bright imagined head of my dark blessing,
step down from your height for me. Yet do not tread
this gross earth with your Ilion-conquering foot.
You slave-girls whom I told to strew his way
with our most costly weaving—do it now.
Now may his paths all merge one crimson red
as Justice brings him unexpected home.
As for the rest, sharp thought that outwits sleep
will work the fated justice the gods keep.

AGAMEMNON

Daughter of Leda, steward of my house,
your speech was like my absence: long stretched out.
The praise I deserve to have should have come from others.

No, do not soften my delicious steps
so womanly with *this*, nor fall and worship,
crying aloud to me like some barbarian.
And do not make me walk this envious way
and draw the waiting wrath down from Above.
These things are honours for the gods, not men.
The man who walks and soils such silken gear—
a fool does this; a twice-fool, with no fear.
I am no god. Give me a human's due.
This sheening scarlet broidure-web I call
no footpath for my trampling to tear through.
God's greatest wisdom-gift is we not fall
into false wisdom we mistake for true.
Living by this thought only quells our fears:
"Call no man happy till he end with happy years".

CLYTAEMESTRA

To me, speak only what seems truth to you.

AGAMEMNON

You know I never muffle my real view.

CLYTAEMESTRA

At the gods' demand, would you have sacrificed this?

AGAMEMNON

I would, on demand of their direct prophecies.

CLYTAEMESTRA

Would Priam victorious have ventured this sacrifice?

AGAMEMNON

Priam would have trashed this silk and not thought twice.

CLYTAEMESTRA

Then what have you to fear but the people's blame?

AGAMEMNON

The popular view is important, all the same.

CLYTAEMESTRA

No man can be great who gives jealousy *nothing* to chew on.

AGAMEMNON

To persist in this word-war's not the part for a woman.

CLYTAEMESTRA

And yet in your triumph, defeat in this is becoming.

AGAMEMNON

You care so much about winning this victory?

CLYTAEMESTRA

Surrender. Be nobler for giving in willingly.

(tempo)

AGAMEMNON

If you say so, then quick: some slave unclasp
these war-boots, my feet's bearers over the ground.
And as I tread these tapestries, I ask
no evil eye from afar may strike me down.
I am ashamed my footsteps should defile
this costly wealth, this silver-weighted web;
but so be it.
       The foreign girl, meanwhile,
bring her in softly. Heaven is a lead-
en unresponse except to gentle kings—
and only those who have to, accept slavery.
I bring her home as first prize in the pillaging;
she belongs to me by the gift of my infantry.

But now, queen, at your word I bow my head.
Like this, through crimson, to my rest I tread.

AGAMEMNON has descended from his chariot, his feet unshod,
and begins to walk slowly across the tapestry.

CLYTAEMESTRA

    There is the sea. What sun could burn it up?
    From cold dark depths I'll fetch your bright red stain;
    your life-warm dye will drench your kingly robes.
    The price, my lord, is high; but with god's help
    we gladly pay. Since when was *your* house poor?
    How many treasure-vestments would *I* tread
    if I was told to by some palace oracle,
    if such acts would bring back that precious life?
    So long as the root lives, there still lives the green
    cool overshade against sun's burning hate.
    So your return here to your palace hearth
    is like a warm spring day that falls in autumn,
    like a breath of summer snuffed in the winter hall
    where Zeus squeezes out the red wine from the bitter grape;
    and thus the house receives back its finished king.

Exit AGAMEMNON into the palace.

    Zeus, you finish all. Bring my prayers their end.
    To what you have waited to finish, now attend.

Exit CLYTAEMESTRA into the palace.

Pheukteon Enteuthen

How could we return to our land of birth?
By what road might we go to reach that place?

The roads of earth range only round the earth;
our feet are earthly dust; earth's dust they pace.

From here to here a ship or horse may run,
but never take you There—beyond the stars,
beyond the many beauties, to the One.

Then set apart these things; *be* set apart;
in blank blind silence and unknowing's night
know and see with new yet old-known sight.

Plotinus, *Ennead* 1.6.8
05.01.21

Sidlaws Benediction

Blessed be God
Blessed be God for ever.

Blessed be God on the burnsides and on the braesides
Blessed be God on the bramble-track,
                              and at the ruined tower
Blest be the God of old kirks and of older abbeys
Blest be the God of hill-forts and stones of power
Blessed be God for ever.

Blessed be God with the incense of resinous woodsmoke
Blessed be God when the sun makes the wet gorse steam
Blessed be God in the silence of fox and buzzard
Blessed be God in the silly pheasant's scream
Blessed be God for ever.

Blessed be God from heath-hills to barley-fields
Blessed be God for wild strawberries in half-tame gardens
Blessed be God in byres and dung-misted farmyards
Blessed be God at the firesides glimpsed through curtains
Blessed be God for ever.

Blessed be God for the airs that are over the Sidlaws
Blessed be God for the waters that run through the Sidlaws
Blessed be God for the rocks that lie under the Sidlaws
Blessed be God for the land and for those who love it
Blessed be God for ever.

Blessed be God in Eassie and in Nevay
Blessed be God in Auchterhouse and Flocklones
Blessed be God in Kincaldrum and Tullybaccart
Blessed be God while the King is upon King's Seat
Blessed be God for ever.

Blessed be God for the sacrifice of creation
Enormity of subtraction from Himself

Rending away, as a rib, from His fullness of being—
Self-gift, self-abnegation foresigning Eucharist—
By his own null-black absence making Space
That grace and savagery, danger and delight
Might co-engender World:

The gift of Him Who Is
This something not him
He who is all in all
And will re-call at last this other side
Immortal bride.

Now, in this one time and this one place,
Break pace:
Breathe in, and know yourself
Immensely loved.

Blessed be God for ever.

15.01.06

Elegy for a Still-Born Child

I

My waving hands and arms
are caught in your searchlight's throb
they paddle away from the whiteness of your noise.

I am inspected by echoes
I am found in an attitude of prayer
my spine my signature tune.

So you may hear my picture,
you may see the sounds you bounce
off my bones or the four palpitating
chambers of my heart:

shadowy prognostics of the day
my monochrome thin frequencies
will bleed themselves into your roar of colour

II

We spend half our lives asleep
hidden from critical eyes
asleep
falling and falling through deeper and deeper seas
spiralling downwards from light to abyssal plains

Asleep
far over the blurry borders of self-knowledge
asleep
in the warm and muffled cradle of the unconscious,
where what cannot and could not be known or clarified
is joyfully grasped as certainty and revelation:
Is it, then, sleep
that gives life its mystery?

To be married is to sleep together
a bond four-fifths of sleep
The lovers' life,
paradigmatically,
is shared unconsciousness

where that can be obtained

III

But there is no sleep,
together or apart,
at midnight or at three o'clock of night,
when the child no longer kicks
and the fluttering of limbs has ceased
in the silent full womb;
this is the night of unsleep.

IV

From an aeroplane, cumulus clouds are seen as dreamt:
dazzling impossible peaks of yellow cream,
top-heavy bulbous spires and onion domes
overtipping and ballooning slow-motion avalanche,
shredded through by our stationary wing-tips.
Could I climb those cauliflower upsidedown mountains,
stand in those noble courts of make-believe,
swim in the foam and steam of that bubble-bath ice?
Is this the realm of the blue-white unicorn,
the cuckooland of the silver prince?
If these are the storybook Heavens,
and if we flee her to find her,
then is she here too?

V

Sun sets, ice sets, mists rise;
wisps of fog to wade through like long grass;
frozen and purpling sky, and the moon's splendour;
a nice new gravestone, and, elsewhere, a man
who is having a succession of electric shocks
put through his balls. Do you understand?

VI

The ferry to Raasay in a dark drizzle
bitter cold night-black waters and
the hulk of Glamaig, remembered from seventeen years;
                    children paddling in rain at Temptation Bay,
and a stone brought back from the end of the habitable
      world;

and the monstrous hospital,
the concrete ogre smoking with children's blood,
still pursuing me over the roofs.

Understanding means tears.

VII

Through the shining hills there runs
in sunlight our child who would have been
but is not and will not be seen
until our bones are meal and there is no sun.

In memoriam
Caitlin Frances Richardson Chappell
17.06.95

Highland Envoi

Before you sleep for good, remember this:

the moss-soft bridge within the dripping wood,
the wild catch of sea air blown on high;

night-climbing up, through ice-storm, to the cornices,
the starlit snow-peak shining in night sky;

the slopes you charged, when young, because you could;
and summer's sunlight on your hills of bliss.

02.04.02

Song for Winter Rain

On the black hill and the brittle wood
on the draggled heron by his unwatched mere
on silent henhouses and unlit farms
the rain pours down tonight
       but not in here.

On the oily roofs of locked-up factories
on the steaming flanks of a ghost-train-vacant bus
on potholed lanes orange-shadowed by springing trees
the rain pours down tonight
       but not on us.

On blackhorse breakers no one ever sees
on what the storm does solely for the storm
on the empty decks of midnight's groping ships
the rain pours down tonight
       but we keep warm.

So rub but briefly at the clammy pane.
Spell jokes and songs; refill the cups again.
Pile high the crammed log-basket: stoke: and let
black hails hiss out their spite in our golden grate.

30.11.96

About the poet

Sophie Grace Chappell is a poet and philosopher living in Scotland. She has published numerous works on ancient Greek philosophy, on ethics, and on friendship. *Songs For Winter Rain* is her first collection of poetry.

The following interview with Sophie Grace Chappell was conducted by Helen De Cruz and originally published on the *Philosophers' Cocoon* blog in February 2021. It is slightly edited and reprinted here with permission.

How long have you been writing poetry and fiction and other non-philosophical writing?

Longer than I've been writing philosophy. The first philosophy I tried to write was *A Theory Of Everything*, a complete metaphysics, a catalogue of all existents, when I was about 9. But that lasted about three pages, and it was a one-off, because I went to the town library and discovered that Aquinas had beaten me to it; most annoying. And before that I had already written lots of non-philosophy.

I had various ambitions as a small child, including joining the "clever men at Oxford" that Mr Toad compares himself to in *The Wind in the Willows*. Specifically, I wanted to be Oxford Professor of Greek. I didn't start wanting, intermittently, to be a Philosophy professor till I was about 16. And even when I did encounter the formal study of philosophy, at Oxford in 1984, one of my first main objections to it as a subject was that it wasn't creative—it was about criticising, not making; it was pulling things apart, not putting them together. As an undergraduate I didn't like that about philosophy; but then, I didn't like it about lit crit either. It took me a long time to see, first, how criticising things is valuable too, and secondly, how, anyway, writing philosophy can be creative. And literary criticism as well.

Whatever else changed, I always wanted to be a writer. So, from the beginning, I wrote. From about 7 onwards, when I read *The Hobbit* and *The Lord of the Rings*, there was lots of sub-Tolkien stuff, both prose and verse, and I invented maps and languages like Tolkien too. My made-up languages were probably better than my made-up worlds. But surely this is one of the main roots of being a writer—parallel in its way to one root of being a musician, I suppose. You read things and you think "That's marvellous, could I do that? Or anything like it?"

Probably it was partly Tolkien's fault, and partly the Lake District's, that as an adolescent trying to write poems I got stuck on the Romantics, all cloud-capped crags and babbling becks and trumpeting torrents. I was, in James Stephen's wonderful phrase, "bleating articulate monotony". I needed, of course, to do something more than mere imitation. And I couldn't find a voice of my own that wasn't sub-Wordsworth or, worse, sub-Tennyson or sub-Tolkien.

When I was in the sixth form, so between 16 and 18, three things unstuck me. One was Mel Shewan, an English teacher at school whose persona was Geordie working-class down-to-earthness. Via Dylan Thomas, and William Blake, and Gerard Manley Hopkins, and Philip Larkin, and Ted Hughes, and R.S. Thomas, and Seamus Heaney, and Coleridge and Keats and Shakespeare and Yeats and, yes, even old Wordsworth and Tennyson, Mel Shewan helped us see that poetry is neither swords-and-sorcery, nor a stuck-up fop in a floppy shirt swooning over a snowdrop. It's elemental, it comes from the dark places within you, from the cellars or Minotaur-labyrinths of the psyche, from the gut. But it's also real, and this-worldly.

The second thing was the Mersey Beat poet Steve Turner, whose sharp, witty, hip, up-to-date, and (again) down-to-earth free verse

showed me that poetry can be completely contemporary, unpreten-
tious, straight-talking, streetwise—and funny, too. (I love comic
verse, and I think in general it's not taken seriously enough. The
best comic poets are never just comic: Michael Rosen, Wendy
Cope, Hilaire Belloc, Betjeman, Kipling, Pope.)

And the third was seeing Tony Harrison's *Oresteia* at the Na-
tional Theatre with my parents—my 19th birthday treat in Novem-
ber 1983. That was one of the two greatest theatrical experiences
I've ever had. (The other was the English Shakespeare Company in
Southampton in 1989, all the history plays, *Richard II* to *Richard
III* in a single day.) Harrison's Aeschylus was a revelation to me of
what a translation from the Greek can be. Again, it's elemental,
it's verse from the gut, studiedly proletarian, very psychically
immediate and powerful. And about as far from Gilbert Murray,
God help us, as it's possible to be.

I've been writing poetry, on and off, ever since. I haven't really
kept up other kinds of non-philosophical writing. There's been
a little writing about mountaineering, but only the odd bit, and
what I wrote when for example I described one particular climb
was really a prose-poem. If that doesn't sound too pretentious.
All I mean is that I wrote to get it across what it felt like to be
there, and to climb that; like most things I write, the narrative
subserves the feel, not the other way round.

I don't think I'm cut out to be a novelist; not sure why, perhaps
because of this prioritising of feel over narrative. When you write
a novel you show, not say, in the sense that you pare down the
description of feeling to let it emerge from the story. And when
you write a film script you keep going past where a novelist stops
paring down and pare down even further, to make space for the
actors and the camera-work to fill back in. It's not like that with
poems; with poems, essentially it's all there on the page. Poems
come naturally to me. Novels don't, and I imagine a screen-play
would still less, if I ever tried to write one.

Maybe it's also a lack of long-distance stamina. Apart from
the translations, my poems tend to be short; if I write something
long, it's probably a philosophy book. On the rare occasions when

I've tried to write a novel myself, what I write never stands up even to my own scrutiny; I reread and I think "No, people don't talk like that or act like that; your take was so naïve, and I'm not sure what's changed since you wrote this, but somehow, now, you know better than that."

Or maybe it's because I don't myself share the rather reverential lit-crit cult of "the modern novel". Of course there are loads and loads of modern or modern-ish novels that I absolutely love: Vikram Seth, Thomas Mann, Virginia Woolf, Steinbeck, Hemingway, A.S. Byatt, Evelyn Waugh, John Updike, John Fowles, E.M. Forster, Kipling, Dickens, George Eliot, Tolstoy, Dostoevsky, Victor Hugo, *Moby Dick*, *Tristram Shandy*... But there are also a lot of modern novels that I'm "supposed" to like but which just bore me. And some of the most canonical novels of all, in particular those of Hardy and Lawrence, I actively detest. It's ideological. Both Hardy and Lawrence, in their very different ways, had quite preposterous world-views, and their novels are nothing without their world-views. There are good novelists who preach, of course. But if a novelist does preach, the reader can only hope that their preaching will be absolutely compelling, like Dickens's or Hugo's; not cloth-eared like Tolstoy's, or ridiculous like Lawrence's and Hardy's. One would, to paraphrase Oscar Wilde, need a heart of stone to read the denouement of *Jude the Obscure* without roaring with laughter. Which at least beats *Sons and Lovers*, where there's not a laugh to be had in all its 350 pages of portentous, lugubrious, tortuous, ill-digested adolescent angst. Can't be doing with it.

Also—the feel/narrative contrast again—the things in modern novels that I do enjoy are very often the lyrical set-pieces: *Moby Dick* is I think the greatest American novel for just this reason, for Melville's fantastic set-pieces.

What have you written?

About 150 short poems, some very short indeed, nearly all of them less than 25 lines long. A handful of translations of lyric poems by authors like Catullus—one of my first loves—and

Horace—whom I think you get to love as you get older, he's so saturnine, so cynical, so funny, so worldly, and so sad.

On a much larger scale, I've written translations of the *Oresteia* and of *Prometheus Bound* by Aeschylus, and of *Aeneid* Book One. I suppose the *Oresteia* is my most substantial achievement as a poet; it was an awesome and humbling experience to live with it for about three years, and I was genuinely sad to complete it. But I have replacements. In fact I'm now engaged in two long-term translation projects at once—the *Iliad* and the *Divina Commedia*. It's a great way to spend the evening. Certainly beats watching TV. Or reading *Sons and Lovers*.

What are the venues where you've published? Do you have links?

In the orthodox sense, I barely have published.   Philosophy is hard enough to get published, God knows, but poetry is much harder.   I've been trying for 30 years... Most of my stuff is already on the internet, though, at `https://www.academia.edu/10435047/Poems`. And here for all the translations I've done—quite a lot of them actually: `https://open.academia.edu/Sophiegrace/translations-of-classical-texts`.

What is the relationship between your poetry and your philosophical work? Is there any connection?

As I said in another interview recently, "Everything I do is connected to everything else." See next answer...

What makes you write a poem?

I think there are four basic reasons to write poetry. First, to create an art-work, an aesthetic object. You want to make something hard, crystalline, resistant, other; something itself, something with a life of its own, something with inscape, as Hopkins would say. And something beautiful, and something permanent: exegi monumentum aere perennius, said Horace, and indeed his work has outlasted bronze. Something that will outlive you. An object that is out there; an objective object. Something that is both very clear—the audience can see at once what it is, what it says—and also in some ways mysterious or opaque: you can't see everything that's there in it at a first look, maybe not even at a hundred-and-first look. It's an icon, it intrigues you, it draws you back, you can't stop thinking about it. In all their very different mediums, the best art-works are like that, I think: rich and strange, both clear and obscure at once, both readily available and strangely self-contained. Each in its unrepeatable way adds something to our reality. And a poet wants to make—another one of those. Only different from every other one that's ever been made before.

Secondly, a poet wants to "limn the contours of reality", in Quine's phrase: to explore what's actually out there, how things really are; to tell the truth. Philosophers and scientists do this too; all three are trying to photograph the same reality; but with different filters on their lenses. (That's why I've never bought the philosophy-will-clip-an-angel's-wings line. It's not that philosophy and poetry aren't in competition because they're not in the same business. In a deep sense I think they are in the same business, especially in exploring our experience of value. But that's all right, because they go at it in quite different ways.)

Thirdly, it's to make an epiphany about an epiphany. You experience something wonderful or great or terrible, and you want to make that experience available to others, to get them to see the thing that you experienced, not first-hand but through the medium of art.

Fourthly, and more generally, you do it to memorialise, to preserve, to express gratitude for good things and to give some shape and dignity and perspective to sufferings and to bad things.

There may be other reasons too sometimes, but certainly these four.

How does it happen when you write one?

As Stephen Fry rightly says somewhere, poems aren't made out of feelings. They're made out of words. So you can have all the lyrical emotion in the world and you won't get a poem until you find an outlet for the feelings: in words.

So there's a form-content gap to close. You have the emotion or the experience or whatever, but you need the words, and the technical skill, and the knowledge of the tradition, of what's already out there, to embody it. So I write down scraps and phrases that come to me, and I read a lot of poetry myself, and I look carefully at the technique of poets whom I love and admire: what's their rhyme-scheme, what metres do they use, how do they unite sound and sense, form and content? And then one day it turns out that I can use that phrase to express this, and doing it like that will be something new, something surprising, something that works, and that no one has ever done before. And once you have a way in—a riff or a hook, as musicians say—you build the rest of the poem around that hook.

You kind of creep up on it, stealthily closing down the form-content gap, bit by bit. And then one day, perhaps quite suddenly, you see it, or you hit on it, maybe without exactly meaning to. You come up with something and you look at it and you slowly realise, ex post facto, the reasons why your subconscious gave you that; there is aesthetic luck involved, no doubt about it. You're trying, like I said above, to make a thing, an art-work, and ideally it will be something quite unlike anything that else that has ever existed. You can't have a plan for doing that; if you did have a plan, the plan would be doing it. You move in the dark, and you see where you get to. That's what it's like to write a poem, for me anyway. Translation is different, of course, and in one way easier: you're given the content, you just have to find the form. Translation is a wonderful exercise, a real privilege, and possibly a sacrilege. It's about trying to do to your readers in English what the poem does to you in the original language. (If only one could translate English poems into English; but there, of course, at any rate since Chaucer, there is something of a barrier.) Translation is an act of homage, at least when I do it. It's not trying to replace Homer or whoever, but to convey what he is to me. An epiphany of an epiphany again.

Who are your influences?

To call them my influences would make it sound like I'm claiming they're audible in the way I write myself. That would be lovely, but it would also be either an admission of derivativeness in the bad case, or a pretty ambitious claim in the good case. But I can speak unproblematically of my favourite poets, the ones I dwell on and take as my masters. And I've already named most of them. I'm very traditional and canonical. In English, Shakespeare is absolutely central for me, and that other great master of the monosyllable, Yeats. Donne and Herbert and Keats and Rossetti and Hopkins and Dylan Thomas and Auden and Eliot and Larkin and Hughes and Harrison and Heaney. In Greek, Homer and Aeschylus and Sophocles and Sappho. In Latin, Vergil and Horace. Then Dante and Rilke and Goethe.

So yes, I'm very traditional and canonical. But I'm also very aware that poetry is deeply democratic, perhaps more so than novels or play-writing because of the relatively low time-cost involved in writing a short lyric. Lots and lots of people write quite wonderful poems, always have and always will; even obscure poets like me. Google "Note" by Linnet Drury, which my daughter Miriam sent me recently. Linnet is 17. She's a schoolgirl in Oxford. "Note" is the best lockdown poem I've yet seen.

Who would you like to read you?

Oh, everybody. And not just everybody who already reads poetry. Everybody everybody. The telos of creative writing, of any writing, is to be read. And also, I'd like to be one of those rare authors who wins readers over to poetry. A lot of people, perhaps the majority, need winning over: they are as resistant to poetry as I am to the modern novel. They say things like "If you want to say this, why not just say it? Why does it have to be all dolled up in rhyme and metre?" Which is like saying "If Darcey Bussell wants to get across the stage, why can't she just walk across the stage, in flats and slacks and a mackintosh? Why the tutu and the spins in the air?" Poetry is to prose as dance is to walking—unless of course the prose is poetical too, as the best prose is. To think of poetry as an amalgam of function and decoration is absolutely wrong. If you accept the distinction between them at all, and you shouldn't, the decoration is the function.

Which poem are you proudest of writing?

Ha! The one I wrote last. When you write a poem it's like laying an egg: you just sit there and gloat over it. At least you do if you think it's any good.

Or maybe I should have said "the one I'll write next". I certainly don't feel that I'm running out. On the contrary, I've barely started. There's a lot to say, and I'm reasonably confident, these days, that I have the technical proficiency to say it, provided I concentrate and make space and stillness in which to write things, without distractions and noises off. And I'm very lucky, because most of the distractions I have to get past are no one's fault but my own, like Twitter.

I don't have one single favourite poem of my own, any more than I have a single favourite poem by any of my favourite poets. But there are about ten or fifteen that I'm particularly proud of, so they were the first to get picked for *Songs For Winter Rain*: "The Box", "Before An Icon", "Song For Winter Rain", "Two Pets", "Elephants", "Music Recalled", "Vigil Of Easter", "Spring Cleaning", some of the lyric translations. I'm very glad I wrote those, and pretty sure that each of them, in its no doubt small way, adds something to the world that couldn't be there otherwise.

How do you balance these activities and your professional life?

I am very lucky, especially during this lockdown; my time is largely mine to command. The way a day usually goes at the moment is, I start by fussing over emails and work admin; then I read for two or three hours (I'm currently reading Plato's *Cratylus* and *Plotinus, Enneads* 3 and Pierre Hadot, *Exercices Spirituels*); then I write some philosophy; then, early evening, I translate 5 lines of the *Iliad* (right now I'm near the end of Book 8) and 6 or 9 lines of Dante (right now I'm in the middle of Canto 12 of the *Inferno*). If I read poetry, it's after that, late in the evening; though sometimes I read poetry first thing in the morning, in bed.

On the days when a poem, an actual new poem of my own, is on the go—which happens about ten times a year—I drop everything else until I've nailed it, or got as close as I can to nailing it.

A life of reading, thinking, and (if I get round to it) writing. It's pretty much what I hoped for as a child, only, like I say, it's philosophy and poetry rather than classics and poetry as I imagined then. I'm a lucky so and so, no doubt about it.

Tell us in a bit of detail about one of your poems in particular.

Well, take "The Box". Obviously, this is about the difference between living by vision and living by routine, and how hard it is to do the first, and how much we lose by doing the second.

Less obviously, perhaps: either it actually is a folk-tale from somewhere, or it really should be—maybe I'm thinking of the fortune-telling in wells and mirrors in Cold Mountain—that if you line up mirrors opposite each other, you will see your one true love away down the end of the infinite regress of mirrors in mirrors. That set me to thinking about the pursuit of the beloved in the mirror, the beloved who always flees and is never to be caught. And that came to seem to me an image of a life of empty, hopeless longing. And of the ways you might try and kill that longing, and of what would be left of you then if you succeeded, or near succeeded. And what it all came to, was this.

You can read "The Box" on pg. 47.

Also available from
Ellipsis Imprints

• • •

• *Heaven Can Wait* by R.J. Davnall

Tom never expected to die young; much less to be met by the Men Who Weren't There upon his death. Who are these Men? And what is the Non-Agency they work for? More importantly, is there any way Tom can make sure he doesn't end up in Heaven? Book 1 of the Non-Agency series mixes humor, bureaucracy, and romance to serve up fantasy story that will appeal to anyone who has ever wondered what life after death is like.

• *Striking Bodies, Striking Minds* edited by Sara L. Uckelman

Stories, poetry, songs, art, and more from the 2018, 2019, and 2020 higher education strikes in the United Kingdom. Proceeds from the sale of this charity anthology are donated to the Universities and Colleges Union Fighting Fund.

• *An Awfully Big Adventure* by Gwen R. Uckelman and Sara L. Uckelman, illustrated by Carolyn Friedemann.

When Maribel and her mother find a starfish on the beach, neither of them expect the adventures that will follow! This charming children's story is sure to delight readers of all ages, and will particularly appeal to young readers ready to advance from picture books to chapter books.

For more information, go to
http://www.ellipsis.cx/~liana/ellipsisimprints/
or visit us on Twitter: @EllipsisImprint